All For The Greater Honor And Glory of God!

MY PUNS ARE A JOKE!

MOSTLY
ASSORTED PUNS

RONN OSIECKI

My Puns Are a Joke!
by Ronn Osiecki

Printed in the United States of America

ISBN 9781624191039

www.xulonpress.com

Introduction

Ronn Osiecki: Received a BPA from Art Center College of Design, Los Angeles, California. He also attended the University of Maryland, Far East Division. When he served in the US Army, he was also responsible for design and design illustration for the 3rd Army Training Aids. He joined Design North, in Racine, Wisconsin as a senior designer and design consultant. He left to form Design Research Unit, USA. He also was a member of the board of directors of the Milwaukee Society of Communicating Arts. He retired with 16 years from The Milwaukee Journal/Milwaukee Sentinel, in promotion, marketing services and creative services. For the last ten years he has been writing assorted puns, truisms, witicisms and proverbs, in his wooded cabin in North Central, Wisconsin.

**SOME OF
MY EARLY PUNS
BEAR REPEATING
WITHOUT BEING
GRISLY!**

ASSORTED

- An inspiring high school English Literature teacher told her class to write 200 words on the Leaning Tower of Pisa as it stands now, but then put a new slant on it!

- As two opposing attorneys took their seats, the lawyer for the defense judiciously pleaded with the prosecutor to get off his case!

- This months oranges for the Wisconsin Produce Market are slightly out of reach!

- Price wise the mattress saleswoman was soft on her last three customers. On the next three she will have to spring for firms!

- Last years flooding is all water over the dam!

- I don't like the looks of that trashy landfill proposal you submitted!

- I thought I'd stay in Anchorage for another winter. That's when I got cold feet!

- What kind of lunch meat are you using on these subs? You won't say? Ok, I'll bite!

- A playground guardian witnessed a minor altercation on a jungle gym between two third graders, but decided to let it slide!

- My eyes were not deceiving me when I saw a lilac violet. Or was it a violet lilac?

- A highly critical symphony orchestra conductor habitually harped heavily on his remiss string section!

- Frankfurter salesmen work in a dog eat dog environment. Never the less, it helps them to bring home the bacon!

- Check it out! That beetle has a cracked bumper. It must have made a lasting hit with someone!

- In harness racing, the trotters and jockeys all try desperately to pull a fast one!

- You can bet that our newly proposed city holding reservoir expenditure won't hold water!

- Because of a major mishap, half of the Eskimo population were forced to go cold turkey this Thanksgiving!

- It was common knowledge that all of uncle Wally's cigarette money went up in smoke!

- During arbitration the Mason's union hit a brick wall!

- In a secluded breakfast nook pancakes were selling like grilled hot cakes without being syrupy!

- In rush hour traffic the lead footed carpenter got nailed!

- I've got to get to work and go to work!

- That circuit court judge is so early, he will have time to sit on the bench in the park and listen quietly to all the nutty squirrels registering their scattered gripes!

- Our giant refractor telescope is the biggest in the world. Come take a look! It's a heavenly sight!

- It's obvious that the ex-con cab driver is still headed in the wrong direction!

- In buying three zealous blood hounds for the police department, the department head ended up paying through the nose!

- When uncle Jones chose a career in truck driving he knew immediately he would be in it for the long haul!

- I had a job with the garbage pickup department, but I had trouble carrying it out!

- I went to see the Grand Canyon. But I was determined you see one, you see them all!

- The collapse of the once solid Concrete Empire Firm was at the end spreading itself much to thin!

- For some, skydiving can be their downfall!

- That bitty, bitty hot dog is a teeny, weeny!

- In our next game of soccer, we are definitely going to get our kicks coming and going!

- That steamed thug is a half baked con in a hot riped off “78” chevy!

- That strike out king has had one to many foul ups! Show him where the bench is!

- It's bound to happen! While starting with a gigantic pile of chips in Reno, Lucky in no time flat blew his stack!

- Any way you look at it the slaughter house butchers were getting a raw deal!

- Just yesterday, I met a jovial meat market butcher who was a natural cut up!

- The entire Science department faculty had good chemistry!

- Our reserve second baseman was going to bat for his injured colleague!

✦ When Michelangelo was not chiseling people out of marble, his nonstop hammering away, in essence, actually made him whole! Another one of his varied accomplishments was to make a lasting name for himself in something concrete and long before he died he made it! When his skeptics were up in arms, he hit the ceiling (really hard)! All his fixed models were said to be petrified! His skeptics also claim he was stoned half the time! Not true! When he was almost finished with the heavyweight Pieta, he still had to figure out how to get a couple of weightlifters to carry it across to the Vatican! Alabaster or whatever it substance was can give a guy a hernia that won't let go! Micky always must have known he had a secondary gift for smoothing things over, including ruptured hernias. He knew in his own mind, but was afriad to even breath it, that blown-up hernias have a way of sticking out like a sore thumb! He, being the sculptor he was, was quite familiar with sore thumbs!

- Just for your information, this years tobacco sales were not up to snuff!

- A Las Vegas card sharks turn to shuffle was no big deal!

- A noted rug designer said to a reputable floor covering manufacturer, "I just developed an alluring magic carpet." The skeptical chairman assurdely said, "I can tell you right off the seat of my pants it will never fly."

- In our men's self-serve clothing store, they told us to feel free to suit yourself!

- If you are way over your head in tillable corn and potatoe acreage, you won't be worth a hill of beans!

- Your fish story line is not easy to swallow!

- Like a fool, I fell for your enticing bait, hook, line, and sinker!

- I don't know how you're able to provide for your family by working in produce on your perishable celery!

- Because of budget cuts at the discount lumber yard management decided to get rid of all the dead wood!

- I understand you're an accomplished clean-cut brain surgeon. Folks claim I've got a spotty mind. Does that automatically make me a candidate for an accomplished, sharp surgeon that can do no wrong!

- The soundproof nursery in the back of the church is a far cry from the previous bawling outs we all received!

- Our newly acquired surgeon is one smooth operator!

- It's a dog life when he's asked to speak!

- By your acting like you're on cloud nine in seventh heaven reeks to high heaven cause everyone knows you're lost in space!

- Just because it's your 60th birthday doesn't mean your going to take the cake!

- You need another power drill like you need a hole in the head!

- Because of shoddy management, the over production of our jersey gloves got way out of hand!

- A newly formed frozen meat patti group had a lot at steak!

- I'll have you know, I come from a long line of genealogists!

- For the amateur, coin collecting just doesn't make a lot of cents!

- I don't think my new boombox will get too heavy for you to carry because its sound alone carries!

- I want one dozen wads of your most resilient packs of Double Bubble gum for a big blow hard acquaintance!

- If you want God to please you then first you must please God!

- I pick up a newspaper every day and the newspaper picks me up every night!

- The newly formed janitorial services business was picking up!

- I read that enticing sky diving school literature, but I'm not going to fall for it!

- Good steaks in Dickyville are rare!

- An aging world class progressive Jazz musician still has a few haunting maladies left inside him!

- Unfortunately and fortunately a magnificently gifted child protege trumpet player loved blowing his own horn!

- A cantankerous male porcupine made his point by needling people!

- For some reason, I misplaced my calibrated hiking compass and now I don't know which way is up!

- Here, take this garlic pill with a grain of salt!

- Because of dwindling passengers, the antique locomotive engineer was somewhat steamed at the promoter. He always thought he was handing him a line!

- Despite my stolen crutches a touching hospital nurse lifted me up!

- If your considering a position as a tower forest ranger be sure to look around first. I hope you're not leery of climbing to the top daily!

- A former homeless field mouse boasted that he now lived in a hole in a wall!

- Family park get togethers are not all picnics.

- If the Indy 500 is not your speed we will go home!

- I just donated six dozen multi-colored yo-yos to the local middle school with no strings attached!

- Just because you're able to work a 500 piece picture puzzle in 4 hours, doesn't mean you've got it all together!

- Attempting three double axels in a row was my downfall!

- I heard twice that Ray Charles could play the piano blindfolded.

- She's got two pair of faulty scissors that don't quite cut it!

- No matter how she slices it, she's going to need new scissors or a scissors sharpener!

- In operating a rifle range, it's pertinent for the proprietor to call the shots!

- It would have been a blessing if before the notorious Chicago fire, Mrs. Oleary's cow would have kicked the bucket!

- 55 thousand fans at county stadium is just a ball park figure! But who's counting?

- I just found a good solution for my cracked chapped hands!

- I can't tell. Are you waiting on customers, or are customers waiting on you?

- 70 home runs in one season! I think you might have hit upon something!

- The resolute mess hall chef, knew how to dish it out!

- Wet concrete mix depth finders, have always been a stick in the mud!

- Although flooded with cars, it's obvious we're not on the right road, but we ARE on the right track!

- You say you and your wife both drive, but I can tell which of you, would never give the other a bum steer!

- My bacon and eggs are peppered and salted. So stop peppering and assaulting them!

- Lap dogBenji, don't go sticking your nose up at the four different kinds of pedigree dog foods I'll be dishing out starting now!

- This basic book on topography should help you and your jeep get over the humps!

- Did you catch wind of that gusty weather forecast? Hopefully it will blow over!

- Take a gander at that immense herd of cattle! Holy cow!

- On any given day things can really get ugly here at our recycling and waste disposal facility. Some people know how to pile it on thick!

- A recovering split personality patient was told to "be her own person" by getting a hold of herself on the double!

- There was a hold up at K-Mart - three price checks in a row! That alone can become a calamitous robbery infringement of time!

- Rumor has it, that the laid back entrepreneur responsible for the success of the Dairy Products Company was the big cheese himself!

- I do not get much of a charge out of owning another additional credit card!

- As far as my new found veggie diet goes, I'm still considered a raw, green vegetarian myself who loves to chew the fat over and over again!

- Because of poor management and budget cuts, the jogging club was slowly slipping on its last legs!

- Three-fourths of the way up Everest the team leader declared, “It’s all down hill from here!” Did I hear him right? (Must be the altitude!)

- The score board clock finally gave out and not a minute to soon! After all, we were all counting on it!

- Freshly fallen snowflakes can’t be matched!

- It is said, the National Aviary is not hard to swallow even for an ardent songbird warbler!

- The once proclaimed drug user is not beating carpets to take out his hostilities. Now, however, his efforts are still way out of whack. But then he could use one himself!

- Did I hear you say you personally trapped eighteen crocodiles? Sounds like a lot of crock to me when in fact it is!

- How can you possibly be a conscientious objector? You've been at war with yourself for years!

- A bona fide fine artist was overheard saying, "The darkest night doesn't seem so bleak with all those alluring little twinkling stars winking at us from heaven a far. I'm inclined to believe they're trying to tell us something in their own quiet way"!

- The devil perpetually insists on raising hell from his hell hole. He's dammed if he does and he's still dammed if he doesn't!

- A little sparrow told me after our Creator master planned the firmament he broke the mold deliberately to save it for us exclusively. What a guy! One of a kind!

- Before we go, perhaps we should get each of the kids an all day sucker to help them stick around all day!

- Appropriately so, an always chipper nordic crack figure skating team decided to break the ice and get on with their ever so slick routine. However, just as a precaution they had cushions to fall back on!

- That nasty Lucifer insists on dragging innocent people down to his own level!

- My last pun is so ridiculous it isn't even funny!

- Purchasing fifty new calculators for the first graders doesn't add up! What's wrong with their fingers? Mine are still good enough!

- A highly qualified (big hearted) heart surgeon explained to his ailing patient that his heart is in the right place. So, stop beating and pounding the life out of it!

- The owner of an ever growing franchise Pet Shop chain was a fat cat who insisted on playing cat and mouse! Till a provoked cat nipped him sharply!

- Even before harvest time three gherkin dill canneries found themselves in a pickle. If you're half pickled to begin with, it's bound to happen sooner or later!

- The gun club shot their mouths off at a gun club practice session after which we all sat around and shot the breeze some more till we couldn't see straight.

- A somewhat clairvoyant was asked, "Did you know that number off the top of your head"? The out of sight clairvoyant said, "Not really. How far off was I?"

- Where are Anna's shoes? Maybe they got legs or maybe they simply skipped!

- Midwinter power outages will continue to burn up frozen residents!

- This is weather for ducks or more explicitly fowl weather.

- Our newly adopted stray terrier is totally lost without her dog tags!

- A convicted lifer thought he'd kill some time playing solitaire in solitary!

- Let's play crack the whip! So do what you can to make it snappy!

- Dr. Nash, my optometrist, declares it's short sightedness at the beach when there's not a single pair of sunglasses in sight!

- Look! There is the meandering trout stream I told you about, that at first sight would appear to be very fishy! (Let's tackle it!)

- Honest to God! One droplet of truth serum is just a drop in the bucket to help you dispense with all the rather fishy fish tales you hypothetically landed!

- If you want Grace to drive you home, give her duty money so the highway fee doesn't take its toll on her!

- I'm curious! How does your soccer player sidekick get his kicks during the off season?

- A disgruntled customer at a thriving fast food franchise couldn't find a plastic hollow tube sipper for his soft drink. That being the case, he demanded to speak to the straw-boss himself so he wouldn't get sucked in by some secondary squirt!

- The entire parish knows quite well, that the custodian that cared for the churches (bell-free) was an absolute ding-a-ling, ding-dong when ever he sounded off!

- I know for certain that six eskimo chieftains sat around all last night trying to act cool by chewing the fat insatiably!

- Your pampered pooch has got you eating out of his hand!

- It isn’t in the cards for me to see my way through in blindfolded pinochle!

- I heard somewhere in our diocese there is a pastor who practices yoga religiously. That doesn’t sound kosher!

- From one beachcomber to another, you owe me 7 horse shoe crabs so shell them out! Half baked is ok if need be!

- A docked air cushion vehicle sailor was recognized by his piers in the sailing industry as a dropped anchor-man

- A newly hired baker apprentice felt he waited much too long for his first raise!

- My car broke down and I needed a lift. But I never dreamed I'd be taken for a ride by a backward cab driver at breakneck speed!

- After laborious months of trial and error, the hula-hoop finally came around in flying colors!

- Today after digging around, I was compelled to weed out some back issues of organic gardening that kept growing in the garage!

- Those deuce and a half military trucks have always carried their own weight!

- This eight lane boulevard is still a two way street for us traffic critics to come down on!

- Two disgruntled matadors got together to shoot the bull. Arena diehards let them have it!

- Turn down that God awful acid rock. That's sound advice.

- That dining room table manufacturer, began turning over a new leaf!

- The cloak room coat thief took the wrap for his needy brother!

- Last years Olympic High Jump winner is certain to win the gold medal again. But lets not jump to conclusions just yet! Let's see how the games themselves get off the ground!

- Just for your own upward lift I got in on the ground floor of the Sears Tower real estate development project! Long before it reached it's lofty peaks!

- You say you want two more Viola bows? I say fiddle sticks to that noise!

- Don't let the lack of fame go to your head!

- The two slender hands from the clock shop that lost face a few minutes ago were last seen punching the clock!

- Look at your six year old youngster. She's going to be a budding author. Just look at the writing on the wall! Have her sign it before it's to late!

- Beat the heat in our completely air conditioned fitness club! We offer our no sweat guarantee!

- Stop the car! There's a fork in the road!

- Brushing my dentures after every meal is like pulling teeth!

- With this concentrated mound of carpenter ants we need to call an exterminator immediately! But till then step on it!

- The chef knew instinctively how to keep his blood from boiling!

- My newly discovered scouring powder turned out to be just another flash in the pan!

- As far as selling men's jeans and casual slacks goes, Jonesy could beat the pants off any salesman in the trouser department. The rest of the staff were determined to hang it up! Maybe they'd be more suited for something more stationary like stationary!

- Some stranger told me in free masonry master masons are given the third degree! Could that be so?

- Several years ago in a celebrity soft ball game David Letterman hit a fly ball right off the bat!

- Two struggling photography students decided to build a dark room just to see how it would develop!

- Our bank doesn't open till nine A.M. Why, what's the hold up?

- Is it possible for a mortician to be the life of a going away party?

- In a preliminary Olympic track meet, a promising gold medal contender had many self-imposed hurdles to overcome!

- Years ago, I knew of a miserly men's tailor who lined his pockets for pennies!

- Would you believe me if I told you I recently saw a billionaire that looked like a million bucks?

- Coincidentally, the fact that our Kindergarten teacher had six boys named Bill in one class gave her the Willies!

- A pathetic hardware inventory clerk has been out of line time and time again!

- Right from the start the poised tight rope walker knew she was on to something!

- It's not unusual for underfed sows to eat like pigs!

- A failing miserably ninety-two year old compulsive gambler recently cashed in his chips!

- Look at the precious white tailed doe carcass lying on the side of the road! (poor dear)!

- That sleazy, wool camping blanket distributor tried to put one over on us!

- I understand your faithful pooch has the patients of a Saint-Bernard!

- For one thing, loneliness is hard to part with all by yourself.

- We're going to light a fire under our landlord with our pile of outdated rent receipts to see if he'll come down to our level!

- Believe me! A two time world class chess master doesn't play games!

- The ship is not sinking! So get off it!

- Aboard a cruise ship, Darwin agreed to purchase a free meal ticket at any price. But, it may cost him considering the pile it on twenty-two coarse gluttonous banquet. With no table scraps to speak of in this case, cleaning off your plate twenty-two times is lustfull and depraved, to put it mildly. As an option, he could consider a half dish of an all dressed garden salad to make him look good!

- I think any psychiatrist or psychologist would agree that most body stress pains originate in your head. So, why don't you open up and use yours?

- That evergreen jack-pine you're sawing is only one half sawn. But, I wouldn't dream of leaning on it while sawing z-zs!

- A first time child went to the barber reluctantly because he had no idea what was coming off!

- They told Sky Queen, the female air head, to go fly a kite and they weren't just stringing her along. They knew she'd get her high and low kicks from the winds sporadic updrafts.

- Can anyone tell me why my Hybrid powered efficiency motorcar, after two years, still won't stop on a dime, for needed fuel?

- I think I'll make another u-turn right here since people are constantly telling me to go back to where I came from!

- If you're unable to appreciate the beauty of a clustered,scarlet blossomed begonia, just sprinkle them lightly daily. They have a way of growing on you!

- As far as she was concerned, Bethel's job, as a lackluster beautician, was a permanent existence! Except maybe, when Beth felt like dyeing!

- The last anyone heard of Amelia Ehrhart was that the fly-by-night pilot was neither here nor there. All her admirers were convinced the gal was totally out of sight!

- Whenever I recalled our problematic leaker plumber, we discovered all his lose fitting work all ended up down the drain. And all because of our inept nonstop up tight plumbing drip!

- A second year asphalt shinglers' livelihood disappeared into thin air overnight. Now he desperately needs some kind of roof over his head to dry out!

- My psychotherapist knows how to bring out the worst in me!

- You took the shirt off my back and then you took me to the cleaners!

- Don't let that cab driver take you for a ride!

- Optometrist says, "I'll take a history on you." There sits a one hundred-four year old woman. She says, "Take your time. You'll probably find me asleep in your waiting room, resting in peace."

- Our platoon First Sergeant, at 4:30 A.M.; instituted a rude awakening to shake up the troops who were still in the dark!

- After my recent gall bladder operation, the administrating surgeon assured me he left no stone unturned!

- Students claim that their high school guidance counselor, Pat Mahoney, was a class patsy!

- By the looks of your seven children surrounding you, it's apparent that you're a-parent of great magnitude!

- Adam and Eve's forbidden fruit fiasco upset the apple cart for ages!

- Did you hear about the police dog that nabbed two fleeing assailants who were asking for it?

- The Friday night dart ball instructor impatiently insisted that of late his prize student was missing the point!

- Perfumed bar soap for sows is a lot of hog wash!

- Eight Natural History museum guides showed a group of forty-two eager beavers how to get around despite declining forests!

- I just heard about the discombobulated street person that misplaced his one and only address book and now is lost without it!

- I heard that one of the stop smoking patch companies, decided to call it quits !

- The costly acquisition of two World War Two mission bombers for the Smithsonian will never take off!

- If you're having trouble bobbing for apples start using your head.

- All of this regions woodpecker population must all be a hard nosed lot!

- Our highway department supervisor actually lives on this road!

- Your Mediterranean dialect is all Greek to me!

- A Swiss artisan watch maker, makes good time fixing second hand watches!

- At our public bathing beach, there were a uniform string of 15 year old floating buoys in the water!

- At an annual fund raising banquet, a radical racist and a pungent cold dinner, left a bad taste in my mouth!

- I heard that attractive optometrist caught your eye before you lost your vision entirely!

- I heard they're going to dig up that cock-eyed racing strip again. Won't that end up being just another one of those straight away drags?

- I heard it second hand that the FBI has over 200 million sets of finger prints just for the record!

- If we don't start pushing our bronze cast personage busts heads will roll!

- If your answering machine isn't working properly you can bet you're not getting the message!

- The last time that counterfeiting engraver went to the bank he had trouble drawing money!

- Some cynics believe the Farmer's Almanac long range forecast is all wet!

- Those slimy medicinal, blood sucking leeches made my moist skin slither in disgust!

- It was obvious there was something fishy going on aboard our tuna trawler.

- For my wife, roasting a twenty pound turkey is pure gravy!

- I wouldn't let that wolf in sheep's clothing (who's been on the lamb for months now) pull the wool over your eyes!

- History has it that Bunker Hill was an altogether up hill battle, except for those heroes who were shot down!

- As to the life expectancy of the stealth bomber, as far as I know, it's still up in the air!

- A leading, big league baseball manager said to his clean up hitter, "try pulling a fast one"!

- Ric-o-chet, a bullet proof firearms distributor, was out gunned by his way out of range nearest competitor!

- A prosperous tree surgeon delighted in dismantling diseased trees, limb from limb, since his business was predominately still climbing!

- I take liberty in saying that pink elephant at the circus was a tusked mastodon of a different color!

- At the resale shop they told me I could have this classical guitar with no strings attached for a song!

- An amateur wallpaper applier when halfway done finally got the hang of it! At one point we almost hung him and gave him a good paste in the mouth for misrepresenting himself!

- I've got so much fishing tackle it's unreel!

- Doc, I don't really have a dislocated femur, do I? You gotta be pulling my leg!

- Our optometrist takes a dim view on non prescription sun glasses.

- In our case, our veterinarian had to look our gift horse in the mouth to see if she was the mouthful we said she was!

- The overweight weight lifter always had strong words for his vulnerable competition.

- I know a landscaper who sold topsoil dirt cheap!

- In Las Vegas there is now a one armed bandit in a laundromat for those who have lost their shirts before!

- When we introduced the 20 some skunk pavilion we unconsciously created quite a stink!

- I'm afraid we no longer stand behind our archery equipment for obvious reasons!

- Consider getting rid of your old, leaky water bed! Give it some serious thought - sleep on it!

- Did you happen to see the classic movie "The Hunchback of Notre Dame"? I'm sorry, but it doesn't ring a bell with me!

- The always thrifty, retiring bank president wanted to save his well chosen words for either his prosperity or posterity. Both would be nice!

- Junior, you say you want to be assigned to submarine duty? Give me a minute, I've got to let that sink in!

- Donald Trump says that every man's home is his castle (he should know) !

- In our one newspaper ad for a exterminator we had responses coming out of the woodwork!

- While in the dentist's waiting room, I thought I heard weeping and gnashing of teeth!

- The stray, rampaging bull was shot, but the question remains unanswered - who shot the bull?

- It's easy to see your tiny bedbugs went undercover!

- In a Federal Conglomerate Bank, an attempted robbery with a toy water pistol didn't hold up. Because of its transparent plastic the tellers could see right through it!

- Don't fret about moving a piano. Your piano will move you in no time!

- I see it's almost six o'clock and the Hallmark Gift Store was wrapping it up!

- Because of all those determined vicious shoppers at the shopping centers, I got mauled to pieces!

- I wonder - does every box of Wheaties have a cereal number?

- The German Christmas cake you baked was stollen!

- My inexperienced massuse rubs me the wrong way. Maybe he'll take a powder instead!

- Go to the pharmacy and pick up a bottle of cough medicine and don't forget to shake it up!

- I'm carrying a torch for a gal in the Winter Olympics!

- The electric light bulb was just one of Thomas Edison's bright ideas!

- A totally deaf, wheelchair plagued robbery victim was missing a lot!

- After Jumbo the Elephant did his job where he shouldn't have, a jumbo fan asked the trainer if he was going to rub his nose in it. The trainer replied: "That would take much to long if you know what I mean!"

- Never let it be said that Sir Francis Bacon, while officiating as Chancellor of England, never lost his head!

- Our hometown optometrist, swore with conscientious devotion: "That our high school Biology teacher had two strange looking pupils"!

- At night, the intense New England Portland Head lighthouse beacon was always beaming!

- The knocked over manual alarm clock was picked up from the floor. But fortunately it was still off and running like clock work!

- How did the escaped leopard get way across town without getting spotted?

- Confucius' brother-in-law always said, "Avoid a dentist with a big mouth. Find one with some degree of lockjaw to make your visit painless as possible."

- Son, here's your new trumpet. Now don't blow it!

- This year's INDY 500 was won by a mile!

- A female accomplished auto upholsterer didn't have to take a backseat to anyone!

- Surprisingly enough, a recent winner of the Kentucky Derby was a thorough-bred dark horse that took his winning in stride!

- An elementary school teacher, insisted that she wanted her pupils to memorize a short list of conjunctions - no ifs, ands, or buts about it!

- All our friends tried to talk my practically tone deaf brother to get one or two hearing aids, but he wouldn't listen to anyone!

- A prominent New York fashion designer promised his stockholders that if his latest jersey top creation didn't sell he would eat his shirt!

- With four minutes left in a tie score championship basketball game, a seven foot superstar got thrown out of the game for being all fouled up!

- Life has taught a poor hurting dentist, who used novocain sparingly, a painful lesson!

- For my first encounter in a trout stream, my fishing buddy insisted that I wear his hip waders till I get my feet wet!

- This new Japanese abacus is not a toy! It's actually something you can count on!

- My part time job at the ham and egger is my bread and butter!

- Laughing hyenas must have preposterous funny bones that have a way of tickling them to no end!

- I just let my twin brother use my brand new radial auto polisher. No sweat, he's one smooth operator! He'll handle it gingerly! On the other hand he could polish it off for good!

- It was rumored that an acclaimed archeologist and his wife had several rare skeletal bones in their closet!

- Teliesin-West, in Arizona, was one of Frank Lloyd Wrights' far out pieces of architecture!

- These dull antiquated sewing scissors don't cut it anymore!

- Tiny, you're always making a big thing out of your Lego's.

- Last night an apprehended, cunning bowling ball thief was black balled from our well illuminated alley!

- At the maternity ward at St. Joseph's Hospital it was normal to have a bunch of cry babies simultaneously!

- Two impudent supermarket check out gals were told emphatically to pack their bags!

- Even for an Arctic region Eskimo weatherman it's bad news to be left out in the cold!

- In bowling circles a bowling ball salesman is destined to carry a lot of weight!

- Believe me, I'm a well trained masseuse and I know how you feel!

- The arson's only fear was getting burned!

- Landlords on both sides of the track had real close boarders!

- Unfortunately, management at the Preservative Works were canning people left and right!

- A brand new airline loaded with a lot of hype was prepared to take off!

- The name of that twenty-four hour cough relief is right on the tip on my tongue!

- Drilling for oil has its ups and downs!

- A dental school intern told his really sore aching patient that after novocain it had to be all in her head!

- When preparing an age old secret canning recipe for dill pickles, a family novice, for some strange reason had a tough time keeping a lid on it!

- A far removed descendant of Louis XV and Louis XVI who is now an antique dealer of period furniture because of his lineage he thought he really know his stuff!

- An accomplished classical guitar tutor was instrumental in the prodigies development!

- While in the UK driving on the left side of the road seems rather backward!

- Yacht Club heavyweight Tubby and I were in the same boat. We both had a tendency to go overboard on suggestive suggestions!

- You'll pay dearly for that paved highway (four years down the road).

- Lap dog Benji's not only a faithful companion, but he refuses to talk back for any reason! Guess it goes without saying!

- Were you aware I'm a sucker for lollipops?

- The previous lackluster Milwaukee Bucks are now on the rebound!

- Did you hear about the slow drip plumber who after thirty years in the business was completely drained?

- If they haven't one, one of the electric companies should adopt the slogan "more power to you".

- This unfinanced section of Highway 13 has always been most difficult for donors to come across!

+ My diet consists of everything from soup to nuts!

+ A second rate sign painter said across the room, "if you want a sofa sale placard, just give me some kind of sign".

+ Rumor has it, that Fredrick Remington, the bronze sculptor, had a way of ironing things out with his statuesque wife!

+ (Kleptomaniacs excluded!) The Lord helps those who help themselves.

+ I've finally got a handle on the scouring fry pan business, but I refuse to rub it in for nobody!

+ A rigid ex-con tight rope walker, for part of his rehabilitation, was prompted to walk the straight and narrow without missing a step!

- The new second hand store will be moving up to bigger quarters. I got that information first hand!

- A good rule of thumb is to not use it for hitchhiking!

- Tailgaters ought to get rear ended themselves to teach them to back off!

- There is never room for a bad apple in the barrel!

- You say I stubbed my toe, I say my foot! I have a bunion or swollen aching toe joint that pains me whenever I try to step on it!

- Baking is as easy as pie or frosting on a three layer cake!

- From the bottom of my heart I must thank my cardiovascular surgeon!

- Without any confirmation an unlicensed bush pilot flew a stolen plane right out of the blue!

- Because of poor attendance in figure skating I, II, and III, Felicity fell through the cracks and froze!

- We call our divine new perfume line a "Heaven Scent". Holy man who came up with that one?

- It's common knowledge that Kowalski, the bulging body builder, lacked strength of character! Have him work on it!

- We've been going over these shredded documents with a fine tooth comb!

- Those tiny sweet valentine hard candy hearts with loving tid bit messages are food for thought. They put words in my mouth!

- After eleven stellar years the circus trampoline act flopped for no apparent reason we can think of! Did they at least give them a elevated uplift?

- A once noted plastic surgeon is no longer raising eyebrows.

- Is that the tacky transparent mending tape you were stuck on?

- I know at least three left handed pitchers that got off on the wrong foot!

- I refuse to say who, but one of our senior vice presidents stepped on a lot of toes while climbing our corporate ladder from the cellar!

- After the circuses' first performance was over all the ringmaster could find to say was "not bad for a bunch of clowns"!

- The peasant that found the Greek statuesque Venus De Milo way back when, must have twisted her arms off to get her out of hiding. (I just don't know what to believe!)

- Someone in our company has been burning the midnight oil. Can anyone cast a little light on the burn out?

- Fortunately for him, that Iowa crop farmer plowed right into our cushioned hay wagon! I would like to know who's going to bail him out?

- After the archaeologist dies you will find that he was an extremely grave man that liked to dig well below the surface to see what would surface!

- When that nasty little runt who constantly irritated the young girls finally got his comeuppance, boy did that pip-squeak!

- I assure you, I know what side my bread is buttered on ever since age three orwas I just flipping for fun!

- I heard of a detergent high jacker that felt compelled to come clean at any cost!

- An overly zealous ballerina taskmaster insisted that his youngsters be on their toes! Till they can't stand anymore!

- For all the head lifeguards cared the gang of bullies could jump in the lake!

- The bridge over the rising Wisconsin River is flooded with suspended cars!

- After laboring steady for 12 hours without a break, a journeyman carpenter appeared deader than a ten penny door jam nail!

- The discovered Christmas candy cane, from approximately 1922, is one tough hard rock crutch not to be reckoned with for all the sweet tea in China!

- Those squawking mallards on the pond are sitting ducks to set our sights on!

- Although piercing for some, for others tetanus shots can get under their skin!

- Grandma Martha's appointment at the hairdresser was all cut and dry!

- Does your tailor shop still do alterations? Yes, we've been known to take 'em in depending on how one looks at it!

- A wedding apparel shop owner said to an apparel clerk, "If you need a tux, tails, and top hat we can help you out, only if you're <u>suitable</u>".

- In the wild west, westward trains often got railroaded. After they abandoned the train and handed the railroaders their distorted railroad line, no one would dare follow in their footsteps if they wanted to remain on the right track!

- At last count, there were twelve priceless pieces of archaic silverware missing from the palace display. So Slippery, I suggest you fork them over while they're still hot and before there hot enough to burn you!

CPSIA information can be obtained
at www.ICGtesting.com
Printed in the USA
BVHW081117071119
563183BV00009B/314/P

9 781624 191039